AF238628

Insta-Brand: The Ultimate Guide to Growing Your Business on Instagram

B. Vincent

Published by RWG Publishing, 2023.

INSTA-BRAND: THE ULTIMATE GUIDE TO GROWING YOUR BUSINESS ON INSTAGRAM

First edition. May 16, 2023.

Written by B. Vincent.

Also by B. Vincent

Affiliate Marketing
Affiliate Marketing
Affiliate Marketing

Standalone
Business Employee Discipline
Affiliate Recruiting
Business Layoffs & Firings
Business and Entrepreneur Guide
Business Remote Workforce
Career Transition
Project Management
Precision Targeting
Professional Development
Strategic Planning
Content Marketing
Imminent List Building
Getting Past GateKeepers
Banner Ads

Bookkeeping
Bridge Pages
Business Acquisition
Business Bogging
Business Communication Course
Marketing Automation
Better Meetings
Business Conflict Resolution
Business Culture Course
Conversion Optimization
Creative Solutions
Employee Recruitment
Startup Capital
Employee Incentives
Employee Mentoring
Followership
Servant Leadership
Human Resources
Team Building
Freelancing
Funnel Building
Geo Targeting
Goal Setting
Immanent List Building
Lead Generation
Leadership Course
Leadership Transition
Leadership vs Management
LinkedIn Ads
LinkedIn Marketing
Messenger Marketing

New Management
Newsfeed Ads
Search Ads
Online Learning
Sales Webinars
Side Hustles
Split Testing
Twitter Timeline Advertising
Earning Additional Income Through Side Hustles: Begin Earning Money Immediately
Making a Living Through Blogging: Earn Money Working From Home
Create Bonuses for Affiliate Marketing: Your Success Is Encompassed by Your Bonuses
Internet Marketing Success: The Most Effective Traffic-Driving Strategies
JV Recruiting: Joint Ventures Partnerships and Affiliates Secrets to List Building
Step-by-Step Facebook Marketing: Discover How To Create A Strategy That Will Help You Grow Your Business
Banner Advertising: Traffic Can Be Boosted by Banner Ads Affiliate Marketing
Improve Your Marketing Strategy with Internet Marketing Outsourcing Helps You Save Time and Money
Choosing the Right Content and Marketing for Social Media Make Products That Will Sell
Launching a Product for Affiliate Marketing
Pinterest as a Marketing Tool
Banner Blitz: Mastering the Art of Advertising with Eye-Catching Banners

Beyond Commissions: Maximizing Affiliate Profits with Creative Bonus Strategies

Retargeting Mastery: Winning Sales with Online Strategies

Power Partnerships: Mastering the Art of Business Growth Through Partnership Recruiting

The List Advantage: Unlocking the Power of List Building for Marketing Success

Capital Catalyst: The Essential Guide to Raising Funds for Your Business

Mobile Mastery: The Ultimate Guide to Successful Mobile Marketing Campaigns

Crowdfunding Secrets: A Comprehensive Guide to Successfully Funding Your Next Project

Insta-Brand: The Ultimate Guide to Growing Your Business on Instagram

Table of Contents

Chapter 1: Why Instagram is the Ultimate Platform for Business Growth

―――

With more than one billion monthly active users, Instagram has quickly emerged as one of the most popular platforms for social media use in recent years. What began as a straightforward app for sharing photos has evolved into a robust platform that has the potential to drive significant expansion for businesses. This chapter will cover the reasons why Instagram is the best platform for business growth and why you should think about using it for your company.

1.1 Instagram is a Platform for Visual Content

Instagram is predominately a visual platform that gives companies the opportunity to present their goods and services in a manner that is both original and engaging to users. Instagram, in contrast to other social media platforms such as Facebook or Twitter, is designed to be a visual platform that encourages users to share images and videos. Users of Instagram are encouraged to share photos and videos. Because of this, it is an excellent platform for companies that sell products or provide services that are visually appealing, such as those that deal in clothing, food, beauty products, or travel.

1.2 Instagram's User Base Is Considerably Sizeable and Active

Instagram has a massive user base that is extremely engaged due to the fact that it has more than one billion active users. Because of this, companies now have the opportunity to reach a significant number of people through Instagram, which has the potential to drive significant growth for their businesses. Because the Instagram algorithm gives more weight to posts that receive a lot of likes, comments, and other forms of user interaction, businesses that publish posts that generate a lot of user interest have the potential to connect with even more Instagram users.

1.3 Instagram Offers a Diverse Compendium of Functions

Instagram provides its users with a wide variety of features that can be utilized in the promotion of their goods and services by businesses. There are a variety of features on Instagram, ranging from Instagram Stories to Instagram Shopping, that companies can use to engage with their audience and propel the growth of their businesses. In addition, Instagram is always adding new features to its platform, which means that companies always have the opportunity to experiment with new ways to promote their brand. This is especially beneficial for businesses.

1.4 Instagram Provides an Option for Personalized Advertising

The advertising platform offered by Instagram enables businesses to create targeted advertisements that are displayed to users based on their interests, demographic information, and behavior on the platform. Because of this, companies now have the ability to create advertisements that can be shown only to those people who are most likely to be interested in the products or services that they offer. Additionally, the advertising platform on Instagram offers a variety of ad formats, such as photo ads, video ads, carousel ads, and ads for Instagram Stories. This allows companies to test out various ad formats to determine which one is the most effective for promoting their particular brand.

1.5. There is a Powerful Culture of Influencers on Instagram

Because Instagram has such a robust culture of influencers, companies now have the opportunity to collaborate with these individuals to promote their goods and services to the platform's user base. Instagram influencers have a large number of followers, which enables them to assist businesses in expanding their customer base and attracting new customers. Additionally, partnering with influencers can help businesses build trust with their audience, as influencers have already developed strong relationships with the people who follow them. This can be beneficial for businesses.

1.6 Direct Communication with Customers Is Possible Via Instagram

The messaging feature of Instagram makes it possible for companies to have direct conversations with their clientele. This enables companies to provide support to their customers, answer questions, and cultivate relationships with the people who follow their content. In addition, the Direct Messaging feature of Instagram enables businesses to send promotions and special offers directly to their audience, which can assist in driving sales and contributing to the expansion of the business.

Instagram, because of its visual nature, large user base that is actively engaged, large number of features, targeted advertising options, strong influencer culture, and direct communication with customers, is the best platform for a growing business. You will be able to expand your customer base, raise awareness of your brand, and fuel the expansion of your business if you integrate Instagram into your marketing strategy.

Chapter 2: Setting Up Your Instagram Business Account for Success

It is essential to create an Instagram account for your business if your goal is to use the platform to expand your customer base. In this chapter, we will go over how to successfully configure your Instagram business account, including the primary features and settings that need to be optimized in order to get the most out of your account.

2.1 Make the Switch to an Organizational Account

Your personal Instagram account will need to be converted into a business account as the first step in the process of setting up an Instagram account for your company. You can accomplish this by going to the settings for your profile and selecting the option to "Switch to a Business Account." This will grant you access to a variety of business features, one of which is Instagram Insights, which provides data on the performance of your account as well as the audience that follows it.

2.2. Select a Photo for Your Profile and a Username

Because your username and profile photo are the first things people see when they come across your account, it is essential to select them thoughtfully. Your username should be easy to remember and reflect the name or identity of your brand, and your profile photo should be of a high quality image that represents your brand.

2.3. Compose an Enticing Biography for Yourself

Your Instagram bio is the ideal location for providing users with a condensed overview of your company and the work that you do. Because you have only 150 characters to work with, it is essential that you are clear and concise in your communication. A call to action, such as a link to your website or an invitation to follow your account, should also be included in your post.

2.4 Please Include Your Contact Information

You should include your contact information on your Instagram profile in order to facilitate communication with prospective clients and make it simple for them to reach out to you. Your email address, phone number, and physical address for the business can all be included here. You also have the option of adding links to your website or accounts on other social media platforms.

2.5. Make Sure Your Link Is Optimized in the Bio

It is imperative that you make the most of the clickable link that you are given the opportunity to include in your Instagram bio. You can create a landing page that links to your website, products, or other content by making use of a tool such as Linktree or Lnk.Bio. Both of these tools are available online. You have the ability to make frequent changes to the link in your bio in order to promote new products, campaigns, or blog posts.

2.6. Choose Relevant Categories

You are allowed to choose up to two categories that most accurately characterize your company when you are setting up your Instagram business account. This helps Instagram understand what your company is all about, and it also gives it a better chance of recommending your account to other users who are interested in the same field as you.

2.7 Take Advantage of Instagram's Insights

Instagram Insights is a powerful tool that gives you data on the performance of your account as well as the audience that follows it. You can find out which of your posts are doing particularly well by using Instagram Insights, as well as the times of day when your audience is most active and the demographics that make up that audience. Using this information, you will be able to create content that is more targeted and therefore more effective.

2.8. Set Up Instagram Shopping

If you run an online store and sell products there, Instagram Shopping has the potential to completely transform your business. You can make it simple for your followers to shop your products directly from your Instagram profile by tagging products in your posts using Instagram Shopping, which allows you to tag products in your posts. You will need to connect your Instagram account to your Facebook Business Page and create a product catalog in order to set up Instagram Shopping.

2.9 Make your own Instagram highlight reels.

Highlights on Instagram are an excellent way to draw attention to the most noteworthy pieces of content and items associated with your brand. Because Highlights are collections of Stories that remain on your profile indefinitely, they are an excellent way to provide users with an overview of what your company or organization is all about. You have the ability to construct Highlights based on a variety of topics, including products, blog posts, or content from behind the scenes.

2.10 Establish Connections Between All of Your Social Media Accounts

Connecting your Instagram account to your other social media profiles is the final step in getting the most out of your presence on Instagram. This enables you to drive traffic to your other social media channels and cross-promote your content across multiple platforms. You can also share your Instagram posts on other platforms, such as Facebook, Twitter, or Pinterest, by using the feature called Share to Other Apps, which is available on Instagram.

In conclusion, creating an Instagram business account is required if you want to maximize the potential of the platform for the development of your company. You can attract more followers, engage with your audience, and drive business growth on Instagram by optimizing your account's key features and settings, such as converting to a business account, selecting a profile photo and username, writing an engaging bio, adding contact information, optimizing the link in your bio, using

Instagram Insights, setting up Instagram Shopping, creating Instagram Highlights, and connecting your other social media accounts.

Chapter 3: Building a Killer Instagram Profile: Tips and Tricks

---

It is essential to make a good impression on potential followers when they come across your Instagram account, and the first thing they will see is your profile, which is located on Instagram. In this chapter, we will discuss some tips and tricks for building a killer Instagram profile, which will help you grow your business on the platform by attracting more followers and assisting you in expanding your presence there.

3.1. Opt for an Aesthetic That Remains Consistent

Maintaining a unified visual style is one of the most important components of a successful Instagram profile. This means that you should use the same color palette, filters, and editing style throughout all of your posts. Maintaining a consistent aesthetic is an effective way to contribute to the formation of a unified brand image and makes your profile more appealing to the eye.

3.2. Utilize Videos and Pictures of a High-Quality

When it comes to building a successful Instagram profile, having photos and videos of high-quality is absolutely necessary. This entails the utilization of high-resolution images and videos that are both in line with the brand and aesthetically pleasing. Your profile may come across as unprofessional and turn off potential followers if it contains images or videos of poor quality.

3.3 Create a Remarkable Personal Biography

A valuable opportunity to introduce potential followers to both yourself and your brand can be found in the bio section of your Instagram account. Create a bio that grabs people's attention and explains your brand's mission and what you have to offer in a way that is crystal clear. You can make your bio simple to read and visually appealing by breaking it up with line breaks, bullet points, or emojis.

3.4. Demonstrate the Unique Personality of Your Brand

Instagram is a visual platform, but it's also a place where users can connect with brands on a personal level. In other words, Instagram is a place where users can connect with brands. Create posts that are genuine, fun, and engaging for your audience to read in order to demonstrate the personality of your brand. Sharing content from behind the scenes, introducing members of your team, or sharing content generated by users are all great ways to foster a sense of community around your brand.

3.5. Tell a Story Through the Use of Captions

Creating a captivating Instagram profile includes the addition of captions, which are an essential component. You can tell a story, share some insights about your brand, or engage your audience all through the use of captions. Make sure to keep your audience interested by utilizing both short and long captions in order to give your profile more variety and appeal.

3.6. Utilize Hashtags

When it comes to expanding your audience on Instagram, using hashtags is one of the most important tools you can use. If you want to reach new followers who are interested in what you have to offer, the best way to do so is to make use of relevant hashtags that describe your brand, products, or services. You could also create branded hashtags in order to encourage user-generated content and increase awareness of your brand.

3.7. Optimize Your Profile Picture

Because your profile picture is the very first thing that people who are interested in following your account will see when they come across it, it is essential to optimize it. Make use of an image of high quality that is both representative of your brand and appealing to the eye. You can also change your profile picture on a regular basis to advertise new services, campaigns, or events.

3.8. Ensure That Your Bio Link Is Always Current

Because the link in your bio is the only one that can be clicked on your Instagram profile, it is extremely important to keep it current. Create a landing page for your website that links to your products, other content, or your website itself by making use of a tool such as Linktree or Lnk.Bio. You have the ability to make frequent changes to the link in your bio in order to promote new products, campaigns, or blog posts.

3.9. Draw Attention to Your Most Valuable Content

Highlights on Instagram are a fantastic way to draw attention to the very best of your content and products. Utilize the Highlights feature to compile a selection of your most compelling posts and provide users with an overview of what your company represents. You have the ability to construct Highlights based on a variety of topics, including products, blog posts, or content from behind the scenes.

10. Interact with Your Audience in Some Way

Last but not least, interacting with the people who follow you on Instagram is critical to the success of your profile. You can interact with other users' posts by liking and commenting on their posts, and you can use Instagram Stories to create polls, quizzes, or question-and-answer sessions. Relationships can be built more easily and there is a possibility that doing so will result in more devoted followers.

In conclusion, developing a standout profile on Instagram is absolutely necessary if you want to increase the number of people following your business on the platform as well as expand it. You can create a visually appealing and engaging Instagram profile that attracts more followers and helps you grow your business by utilizing these tips and tricks, such as choosing a consistent aesthetic, using high-quality images and videos, crafting an eye-catching bio, showcasing your brand's personality, using captions to tell a story, utilizing hashtags, optimizing your profile picture and bio link, highlighting your best content, and engaging with your audience. Keep in mind that your Instagram profile is frequently the first point of contact between your brand and potential followers. Because of this, it is essential to make a positive impression and highlight the best qualities of your brand.

Chapter 4: Creating a Cohesive Aesthetic for Your Brand on Instagram

———

Developing a strong brand identity on Instagram requires first establishing a visual style that is consistent throughout your account. Your brand's image can be more easily recognized, and your profile can look more appealing to the eye, if you maintain a consistent aesthetic. In this chapter, we will go over some helpful hints and suggestions for establishing a recognizable and consistent aesthetic for your brand on Instagram.

4.1 Pick a Color Scheme for Your Website

Picking out a color scheme is one of the first things you should do when you're trying to establish a consistent look and feel for your brand on Instagram. Your brand's personality and values should be reflected in the color palette you choose, and that palette should be used consistently throughout all of your posts. When you use the same color palette throughout your profile and other marketing materials, it helps create a unified brand image and makes your profile more visually appealing.

4.2. Use Consistent Filters

Utilizing the same filters for all of your brand's Instagram photos is another important step in developing a unified aesthetic for your account. Pick a filter that goes well with your color scheme, and make it a habit to apply that filter to each and every one of your posts. By applying the same filter to all of your photos, not only will your profile look more put together, but it will also be more visually appealing.

4.3 Stay True to Your Theme

Maintaining a consistent aesthetic for your brand on Instagram requires that you adhere to a particular theme consistently. Your theme should be consistent throughout all of your posts, and it should reflect the values that your brand stands for. For instance, if you run a fashion brand, you might want to concentrate on posting "outfit of the day" photos or "flat lays" of your various products.

4.4 Design Graphics for Your Company's Brand

The creation of branded graphics is an additional method for developing a unified visual identity for your brand on Instagram. Templates for quotes, product launches, and promotional graphics can all be included in branded graphics. Create a unified look and feel by drawing inspiration from the color palette and fonts established for your brand.

4.5. Employ Lighting That Is Consistent

When it comes to developing a unified aesthetic for your brand on Instagram, using consistent lighting is an essential component. Ensure that your photographs have adequate lighting, and whenever possible, shoot them in natural light. Maintaining the same level of lighting throughout your profile contributes to the creation of a unified appearance and atmosphere, and it also makes your profile more visually appealing.

4.6. Prepare a Feeding Plan

Developing a strategy for your Instagram feed is one of the most important steps in developing a unified visual identity for your brand on Instagram. Utilize a scheduling application such as Planoly or Later to organize your future posts in advance and get a preview of how they will appear on your profile as a whole. This helps to ensure that the aesthetic of your brand is maintained throughout your posts and that they are consistent.

4.7. Play around with the Instagram Stories feature

An additional method for developing a visually consistent aesthetic for your brand on Instagram is to play around with the features of Instagram Stories. You can create visually appealing Stories that reflect the personality of your brand and the values it upholds by making use of templates, stickers, and filters. Create a unified look and feel by sticking to the same color palette and fonts throughout the entire project.

4.8. Edit Your Photographs On A Regular Basis

Another essential component of developing a unified aesthetic for your brand on Instagram is maintaining a consistent editing style across all of your photos. Create a unified look and feel by editing the photo with a method that is consistent throughout, such as by making adjustments to the brightness, contrast, or saturation. When editing your photos in a consistent manner, editing apps such as VSCO or Lightroom should be used.

4.9. Make Use of Content Generated by Users

Utilizing user-generated content is yet another method for developing a unified look and feel for your brand's Instagram account. Encourage the users who follow you to post pictures or videos of themselves using the branded hashtags you've created or by tagging your company in the posts they make. You can generate a sense of community around your brand by showcasing your products or services through user-generated content and using that content.

4.10 Always Remain Faithful to Your Company's Identity

Last but not least, maintaining consistency with the identity of your brand is critical to the development of a unified aesthetic for your brand on Instagram. Your brand's identity ought to be reflected in every aspect of your profile, from your bio to your posts to your Stories, and this obligation extends all the way down to Instagram. Create a consistent look and feel for your brand's Instagram account by letting the values, personality, and voice of your company serve as your guide.

To summarize, developing a visually consistent aesthetic for your brand on Instagram is critical to the process of developing a powerful brand identity and attracting a greater number of followers. You can create a visually appealing and cohesive brand image on Instagram by using these tips and tricks, such as choosing a color palette, using consistent filters, sticking to a theme, creating branded graphics, using consistent lighting, planning your feed, experimenting with Instagram Stories, editing your photos consistently, using user-generated content, and remaining true to the identity of your brand. Keep in mind that a unified design aesthetic not only makes your profile more visually appealing but also contributes to the creation of a recognizable brand identity. This, in turn, can help you grow your business on the platform by attracting more followers.

Chapter 5: Crafting Captions That Convert: How to Write for Engagement and Sales

―――

When it comes to developing a successful post for Instagram, captions are an essential component. It is essential to the growth of your business on the platform that you craft captions that attract the attention of your audience and drive sales. In the following section, we will go over some helpful hints and pointers for composing captions that convert well on Instagram.

5.1. Be Aware of Your Target Market

When it comes to writing Instagram captions that convert, knowing your audience is absolutely necessary. Your captions should speak directly to your target audience and address any issues or interests that are important to them. Make sure that the language and tone you use is one that your audience can relate to and that reflects the character of your brand.

5.2. Recount an Experience

On Instagram, one of the most effective strategies for engaging your audience and driving sales is to tell a story. You can tell the story that lies behind your brand, products, or services by using your captions. Your audience will feel more connected to you and your brand will come across as more approachable as a result of this.

5.3. Use Emojis

You can give your captions more personality and make them more visually appealing by using emojis, which is a fun and effective way to do both. Emojis should be used in a way that reflects the personality and tone of the brand and should also be relevant to the content of the post.

Use a Call to Action (Point 5.4)

When writing captions for Instagram posts with the goal of increasing conversions, it is critical to include a call to action (CTA). Your call to action (CTA) needs to be understandable and succinct, and it needs to motivate your audience to take some sort of action, such as visiting your website, purchasing your products, or following your account.

5.5. Remember to Keep It Simple and Sweet

When you want to engage your audience on Instagram, it's important to keep the captions you use brief and to the point. Because most users quickly scroll through their feeds, the captions you use should be straightforward and simple to understand. Aim to keep the length of your captions to no more than two or three sentences.

5.6. Use Hashtags

When developing Instagram captions with the goal of increasing conversions, the use of hashtags is an absolutely necessary component. If you want to reach new followers who are interested in what you have to offer, the best way to do so is to make use of relevant hashtags that describe your brand, products, or services. You could also create branded hashtags in order to encourage user-generated content and increase awareness of your brand.

5.7. Be Sure to Include Product Specifics

When promoting a product on Instagram, it is important to include specifics about the product in the captions of your photos. This can include information about the price, when it will be available, and the features. When you include product details in your captions, it helps to make them more informative and it can drive sales.

5.8. Ask Questions

On Instagram, one of the most effective ways to engage your audience and encourage them to interact with your brand is to pose questions to them. Make use of questions that are pertinent to the content of your post and that encourage the readers of your post to share their ideas or viewpoints with you.

5.9 Make Use of Laughter

You can make your captions more interesting, engaging, and memorable by using humor, which is a fun and effective way to do so. Make use of humor that is pertinent to the personality and tone of your brand and that is appropriate for the audience you are addressing.

5.10 Editing and Checking for Errors

Last but not least, it is critical to edit and proofread your captions before posting them on Instagram in order to craft captions that convert. Make sure that your captions do not contain any errors, that they are simple to read and comprehend, and that they are in line with the tone and personality of your brand.

When it comes to expanding your business on Instagram, one of the most important things you can do is work on crafting captions that engage your audience and drive sales. You can generate Instagram captions that convert by utilizing the aforementioned strategies, which include knowing your audience, telling a story, utilizing emojis, utilizing a call to action, keeping it short and sweet, utilizing hashtags, including product details, asking questions, utilizing humor, and editing and proofreading your work. These strategies will assist you in achieving your business goals on the platform. Keep in mind that captions present a priceless opportunity to interact with your target demographic and stimulate sales; therefore, you should make the most of these opportunities.

Chapter 6: Hashtag Strategy: Finding and Using the Right Ones for Your Business

―――

When it comes to expanding your audience on Instagram, using hashtags is one of the most important tools you can use. If you use the appropriate hashtags, you may be able to attract new followers who are interested in the things you have to offer. In this chapter, we will go over some helpful hints and pointers for locating and utilizing the appropriate hashtags for your company's Instagram account.

6.1. Conduct Research on Hashtags That Are Relevant

The first thing you need to do when developing a hashtag strategy for your company's Instagram account is conduct research on relevant hashtags. To discover hashtags that are pertinent to your brand, products, or services, you can make use of applications such as Hashtagify or All Hashtag. Look for hashtags that have a high number of posts and engagement but are not overly crowded with other users' content.

6.2. Develop Hashtags for Your Brand

Another strategy for expanding your audience on Instagram is to develop your own branded hashtags. Hashtags specific to your brand are known as branded hashtags, and they can assist in the promotion of brand awareness as well as user-generated content. To create a branded hashtag, you can use your company's name, a tagline, or the name of a specific campaign.

6.3. Make Use Of Hashtags That Are Based On Location

On Instagram, one of the most effective ways to reach a local audience is to make use of location-based hashtags. If you want to attract local followers who are interested in what you have to offer, you should use hashtags that are unique to your city or region. You can also promote events or special promotions by using hashtags based on the location of the event.

6.4. Combine Popular Hashtags with Other Types of Hashtags

When trying to reach a large audience on Instagram, it is essential to use a combination of popular and niche hashtags. Hashtags like #love and #instagood are examples of popular hashtags that have a lot of posts and a lot of engagement, but they also have a lot of competition. The number of posts and engagement that are generated by niche hashtags, such as #veganfitness and #interiordesignideas, is typically lower; however, these hashtags are more specifically geared toward the interests of their users.

6.5 Always Include Hashtags in Your Instagram Bio

When you include hashtags in your Instagram bio, you open up a valuable opportunity to promote your brand and gain new followers on the platform. Users will have a much easier time finding your account if you make use of hashtags that accurately describe your brand, products, or services. In order to promote user-generated content and increase engagement with your profile, you can also include branded hashtags in your bio.

6.6. Evaluate the Effectiveness of Your Hashtag

It is essential to evaluate the performance of your hashtags before attempting to improve your hashtag strategy on Instagram. You can see which of your hashtags are generating the most engagement and new followers by using Instagram Insights to track the performance of your hashtags. To achieve the best possible outcomes, you should adjust your hashtag strategy in light of your performance data.

6.7. Don't Overdo It

On Instagram, using an excessive number of hashtags can make your post appear overwhelming and spammy. Your goal should be to use 5-10 relevant hashtags for each post in order to maintain a clean and easy to read caption. A post's visibility in the algorithm may also be reduced if it contains an excessive number of hashtags.

6.8 Make Use of Hashtags When Posting to Instagram Stories

You can gain new followers and expand your audience on Instagram by using hashtags in Instagram Stories. This is an additional way to use the platform. Make use of hashtags that are pertinent to the content of your Story and that describe your brand, the products you offer, or the services you provide. In addition, you have the option of developing branded hashtags for use in your Stories in order to promote user-generated content.

6.9 Get involved in various hashtag competitions.

On Instagram, taking part in hashtag challenges is a way to grow your audience in a way that is both enjoyable and effective. Participate in challenges that are pertinent to your brand or industry by using hashtags that are relevant to those challenges. Hashtag challenges are a fun way to engage your followers and raise awareness of your brand at the same time.

10. Always Make Sure That Your Hashtag Strategy Is Current

Lastly, if you want to maintain your relevance on Instagram, you need to ensure that your hashtag strategy is always up to date. Conduct research on new hashtags on a regular basis, evaluate the data you've collected on your performance, and adjust your strategy accordingly. Maintaining your awareness of the most recent fashions and hashtags on the platform can help you stay one step ahead of the competition and grow the size of your audience there.

In conclusion, developing a hashtag strategy for your business is absolutely necessary if you want to see growth on Instagram. You can create a hashtag strategy that helps you reach new followers and grow your audience on Instagram by making use of these tips and tricks, such as researching relevant hashtags, creating branded hashtags, using location-based hashtags, mixing popular and niche hashtags, using hashtags in your bio, analyzing your hashtag performance, not overdoing it, using hashtags in Instagram Stories, participating in hashtag challenges, and keeping your hashtag strategy up to date. Keep in mind that hashtags are an important tool for expanding your audience on Instagram; consequently, you should dedicate some of your time to researching and refining your hashtag strategy in order to achieve the best possible results on the platform.

Chapter 7: Creating Engaging Instagram Stories: How to Stand Out from the Crowd

Your ability to engage your audience and promote your brand on Instagram can be significantly boosted by using Instagram Stories. Because there are more than 500 million people using Instagram on a daily basis, it is essential to produce engaging and memorable Stories that distinguish themselves from the competition. In this section, we will go over some helpful hints and pointers for making engaging content for Instagram Stories.

7.1. Make Use of Visuals That Captivate the Audience

When it comes to developing engaging Instagram Stories, the utilization of visually appealing content is absolutely necessary. Make use of high-quality images and videos that are pertinent to your company or the message you want to convey. Make your Stories more visually appealing by shooting them from interesting angles, using vivid colors, and applying distinctive filters.

Stickers and GIFs are highly recommended.

Adding personality to your Instagram Stories in a way that is both fun and effective is to make use of stickers and GIFs. Utilize stickers that are pertinent to your brand or the message you are trying to convey, such as location stickers, product stickers, or emoji stickers. Make your Stories more entertaining or unique by including GIFs in them.

7.3 Take Advantage of the Interactive Features

The creation of engaging Instagram Stories relies heavily on the utilization of various interactive features. Use features like polls, quizzes, or questions to encourage your audience to interact with your brand. Increased engagement and brand awareness are both possible outcomes of incorporating interactive features.

7.4 Make Effective Use of the Text

When it comes to communicating your message on Instagram Stories, one of the most important things you can do is use text effectively. Make use of brief, succinct text that is straightforward and simple to read and comprehend. Make sure that the fonts and colors you use are in line with the overall feel and personality of your brand.

7.5. Make Sound Use of

The incorporation of sound is a crucial part of developing engaging content for Instagram Stories. Make use of tunes or sound effects that are pertinent to your brand or the message you want to convey. Make your Stories accessible to all users, including those who are deaf or hard of hearing, by including captions or subtitles underneath the video.

7.6. Outline the Course of Your Story

Establishing a game plan for the progression of your story is an essential step in the process of creating engaging Instagram Stories. Make sure that your stories have a beginning, a middle, and an end by planning them out in advance with a program like Planoly or Later, which can help you do this. Keeping your stories well-organized and interesting requires careful planning of their arcs.

7.7. Exhibit Your Goods or Services

When it comes to promoting your brand on Instagram Stories, one of the most effective strategies is to highlight your products. Make use of product stickers or tags to demonstrate how your wares can be utilized. Make use of quick videos or images to bring attention to the features and benefits of your product.

7.8. Include Footage from Behind the Scenes

Providing your audience with a glimpse into the personality and values of your brand can be accomplished in an entertaining and productive manner by using footage from behind the scenes. You can demonstrate the creative process that your team or your brand goes through by using short videos or images. Creating a connection with your audience and promoting brand loyalty can be aided by the use of footage from behind the scenes.

7.9 Leverage Content Generated by Users or Content Created by Influencers

Engaging content for Instagram Stories can also be created by utilizing content generated by users or content created by influencers. When promoting your goods or services, it is a good idea to work together with influential people who are in some way connected to your company or industry. Make use of content that was generated by users to highlight your brand's community and increase awareness of your brand.

7.10 Conduct a Self-Evaluation of Your Efforts

It is essential to evaluate the performance of your Instagram Story in order to improve your strategy on Instagram. Make use of Instagram Insights to monitor how well your Stories are performing and to determine which of them are generating the most engagement and new followers. To achieve the best possible outcomes, you should adjust your approach in light of your performance data.

When it comes to promoting your brand and expanding your audience on Instagram, one of the most important things you can do is create Instagram Stories that users find engaging. You can create engaging and memorable Instagram Stories that help you achieve your business goals on the platform by using these tips and tricks, such as using eye-catching visuals, using stickers and GIFs, using interactive features, using text effectively, using sound, planning your Story arc, showcasing your products, using behind-the-scenes footage, using influencers or user-generated content, and analyzing your performance. In addition, you can use these tips and tricks to make your Instagram Stories interactive and interactive features. Keep in mind that Instagram Stories offer a valuable opportunity to connect with your audience and promote your brand. Because of this, you should take the time to plan and create Stories that distinguish themselves from the rest of the crowd and leave a long-lasting impression on your followers. Instagram Stories have the potential to become a powerful tool for expanding your business on the platform if you employ the appropriate strategy and approach.

Chapter 8: Growing Your Following on Instagram: Organic vs. Paid Methods

———

Increasing the number of people who follow you on Instagram is one of the most important things you can do to promote your brand and achieve your business goals on the platform. Organic and paid growth of a user's following are the two primary approaches that can be taken on Instagram. In this chapter, we will discuss the benefits and drawbacks of both approaches, as well as provide advice on how to increase the number of people who follow you on Instagram.

8.1 Methods Using Organic Materials

When we talk about growing our following on Instagram using "organic methods," we mean doing so without using any paid advertisements. Although organic methods require more time investment, they are more likely to result in a following that is actively engaged and committed to the platform.

Pros:

Organic methods contribute to the development of a dedicated and active following on Instagram, which helps build a loyal following. This has the potential to result in higher engagement rates as well as more successful promotions and sales.

increases brand awareness Using Instagram in such a way that relies on organic methods can help increase brand awareness. Your brand has the potential to gain new followers who are interested in the products or services you provide if it generates content of a high quality and uses hashtags that are pertinent to the conversation.

Cost-effective: Using organic methods can be done for very little to no money, yet they still provide excellent results. Because of this, they are an appealing choice for individuals or smaller businesses that want to increase the number of followers they have on Instagram.

Cons:

In order to see results, using organic methods can be time-consuming and requires consistent effort and dedication.

Slow growth: Instagram users who use organic methods may experience slower growth as a result. Building a substantial following through the use of only organic methods can take several months, or even several years.

Organic methods have a more restricted application area than conventional ones. Because they rely on your posts and hashtags to draw in new followers, this can restrict the amount of people you can reach through the platform.

Suggestions for Increasing the Size of Your Audience Using Organic Methods:

Develop content of a high quality that is pertinent to your company's sector of the market.

Make use of hashtags that are pertinent to your business in order to bring in new followers who are interested in what you have to offer.

Maintain a conversation with your audience by answering their questions and addressing their comments.

Engage in joint ventures with competing brands or key opinion leaders in your sector.

Maintain a regular posting schedule and distribute content at times that work best for your audience.

8.2. Paid Methods

The term "paid methods" refers to the practice of using Instagram's paid advertising platform to grow your following. The use of paid methods, while potentially useful for rapidly expanding your following on the platform, does require an investment of financial resources.

Pros:

Rapid expansion: Paid methods offer the potential for rapid expansion on Instagram. You can expand your reach to a larger audience and gain new followers who are interested in what you have to offer if you make use of paid advertising.

Paid methods on Instagram give you the ability to target a specific audience, and you can pay for that ability. This can help ensure that users who are most likely to be interested in your brand or products see your promotions and increases the likelihood that they will.

Results that can be measured are something that can be gained from using paid methods. You are able to monitor the effectiveness of your advertising and modify your approach in response to the data you collect.

Cons:

Paid methods require a budget, and depending on the advertising goals you want to achieve and the audience you want to reach, the cost of these methods can vary widely.

Ad fatigue is a condition that can affect your audience and can be caused by paid advertising. This could result in a decrease in the percentage of people engaging with your promotions and a reduction in their overall effectiveness.

Following that is less committed: Using paid methods can result in a following that is less committed on Instagram. Users who follow your account as a result of paid advertising may have a lower level of engagement with your brand, and they may be less likely to become loyal customers or make additional purchases.

Advice on How to Make the Most of Paid Advertising on Instagram:

Before you begin developing your advertising campaigns, you should first determine your advertising goals and your target audience.

When promoting your company or its products, make use of eye-catching visuals and concise messaging.

When creating your advertisements, it is important to make use of pertinent hashtags and calls to action in order to encourage engagement and conversions.

Keep an eye on how well your advertisements are performing, and adapt your approach accordingly.

Try out a few different types of advertisements, such as Stories and Reels, to see which one resonates most strongly with your target market.

In conclusion, growing your following on Instagram can be accomplished successfully through the use of both organic and paid methods. You can develop a strategy that is optimal for your brand and that assists you in achieving your business goals on the platform by making use of the hints and tips that have been provided, such as the creation of high-quality content, the utilization of pertinent hashtags, the engagement with your audience, the utilization of paid advertising to target a specific audience, and the monitoring of your performance data. Keep in mind that increasing the size of your following on Instagram requires time, effort, and commitment. It is important to maintain consistency and engage with your followers, regardless of whether you choose to use organic or paid methods, in order to build a following that is both loyal and engaged on the platform.

Chapter 9: Collaborating with Influencers on Instagram: Finding the Right Fit

O n Instagram, a popular strategy for promoting your brand and reaching a larger audience through the platform is to work together with Instagram users who have a large following known as "influencers." Influencers are people who have a large number of followers who listen to what they have to say because they are highly engaged and interested in what they have to say. These followers have the ability to promote your products or services to those followers. In this chapter, we will go over some helpful hints and pointers for collaborating with influencers on Instagram as well as finding users who are a good match for your brand.

9.1 Establish the Criteria for Your Influencers

The first thing you need to do in order to find the right fit for your brand is to define the criteria for your influencers. Think about things like the niche that the influencer operates in, the demographics of their audience, the engagement rates, and their overall aesthetic. You should look for influencers whose values are compatible with those of your brand and who have an audience that is comparable to yours.

9.2 Conduct Research on Possible Swayers of Opinion

It is essential to conduct research on potential influencers in order to find users who are a good fit for your brand on Instagram. Analyzing the engagement rates, audience demographics, and overall performance of influencers on a platform can be done with the assistance of third-party applications such as HypeAuditor and FollowerWonk. You should search for influencers who have a following that is genuine and a high engagement rate.

9.3 Make Contact with Possible Influencers in Your Field

The following step in collaborating with Instagram influencers is to make contact with potential influencers in the target audience. Send personalized messages to the influencers you've determined to be in alignment with the core values of your brand and to have met your criteria. Make sure that your expectations and objectives for the collaboration are crystal clear.

9.4. Engage in Discussions Regarding the Terms of the Collaboration

It is important to negotiate the terms of the collaboration in order to ensure that both parties are on the same page regarding their expectations and goals for the collaboration. Define the parameters of the collaboration, including its scope and duration, as well as any compensation or incentives that will be offered to the influencer.

9.5. Develop Content That Is Engaging

It is essential to develop content that users will find interesting if you want to get the most out of your collaborations with Instagram influencers. Collaborate with the influencer to develop content that reflects the core beliefs of your company and promotes the products or services you offer in an original and interesting way. To increase engagement and conversions, it is important to include calls to action as well as images and videos of a high quality.

9.6. Encourage Participation in the Collaboration

For the collaboration to have the greatest possible impact on Instagram, promotion of it is essential. When promoting the collaboration on Instagram, make use of the appropriate hashtags and tags. Encourage the influencer and their followers to interact with your brand and share their experiences with the products or services you offer by providing incentives.

9.7. Conduct an Analysis of the Results

It is absolutely necessary to conduct an analysis of the results of your collaboration in order to perfect your influencer strategy on Instagram. You can track the success of your collaboration by using Instagram Insights or other third-party tools. This will allow you to determine which influencers and pieces of content are generating the most engagement and leading to the most conversions. To achieve the best possible results on the platform, you should adjust your strategy in light of your performance data.

In conclusion, collaborating with Instagram users who have a large following and a significant amount of influence can be an effective method for promoting your brand and reaching a larger audience on the platform. You can find the right fit for your brand and create successful collaborations that help you achieve your business goals on the platform by utilizing these tips and tricks, such as defining your influencer criteria, researching potential influencers, reaching out to potential influencers, negotiating the terms of the collaboration, creating engaging content, promoting the collaboration, and analyzing the results. It is important to keep in mind that the key to a successful collaboration with an influencer is to find an influencer whose values align with those of your brand and who has a highly engaged and authentic following.

Chapter 10: Leveraging Instagram Ads to Boost Your Business

———

When it comes to expanding your reach and promoting your brand on Instagram, one of the most effective tools at your disposal is Instagram Ads. You can connect with potential customers and drive conversions for your business with the help of Instagram Ads. Instagram has more than one billion monthly active users. In this chapter, we will go over some helpful hints and pointers for maximizing the potential of Instagram Ads for your company.

10.1. Outline Your Objectives for Advertising

The first thing you need to do in order to create successful Instagram ads is to define your advertising goals. Think about the goals you have for your advertising campaign, such as raising people's awareness of your brand, attracting more visitors to your website, or promoting a new product. Defining your goals allows you to develop an advertising strategy on the platform that is more targeted and therefore more effective.

10.2. Select the Format of Your Ad

When developing successful Instagram ads, selecting the appropriate ad format is an essential step. Instagram users have the option to choose from a number of different ad formats, such as photo ads, video ads, carousel ads, and Stories ads. Pick the format that works best for achieving the objectives you have set for your advertising and reaching the people you want to reach.

10.3 Make Content That Is Interesting To Read

Making content that people want to interact with is absolutely necessary if you want to get the most out of your Instagram ads. Make use of images or videos of a high quality that are pertinent to your brand or the message you want to convey. In order to encourage engagement and conversions, it is important to use eye-catching visuals, clear messaging, and calls to action.

10.4. Aim Your Message at the Appropriate Audience

It is essential to target the appropriate audience in order to guarantee that the appropriate people will view your Instagram advertisements. Utilize the options provided by Instagram's targeting menu to narrow your focus on users according to demographics, interests, behaviors, and other factors. It is possible to increase the likelihood that users who are likely to be interested in your brand or products will see your advertisements by carefully targeting the appropriate audience.

10.5. Use Relevant Hashtags

It is essential to use hashtags that are relevant to your posts in order to increase the reach of your Instagram ads. Make use of hashtags that are pertinent to your company or the message you are trying to convey and that your ideal customers are likely to look for on the platform. Employ a combination of widely used and more specialized hashtags to attract the attention of more people.

10.6. Evaluate, Analyze, and Improve Your Performance

It is essential to monitor and improve your performance in order to maximize the effectiveness of your Instagram ads. You can track the performance of your ads by using Instagram Insights or other third-party tools. This will allow you to determine which ads are leading to the most engagement and conversions. To achieve the best possible results on the platform, you should adjust your strategy in light of your performance data.

10.7. Take Advantage of Instagram's Advertising Features

You can make your Instagram ads more powerful by taking advantage of the many advertising features that Instagram provides. Utilize Instagram features such as Shopping, which enables users to shop directly from your advertisements, as well as Reels, which can help your advertisements stand out more prominently on the platform.

To summarize, making use of Instagram Ads is one of the most important steps you can take toward promoting your brand and accomplishing your business goals on the platform. You can create successful Instagram Ads that help you reach a larger audience and drive conversions for your business by using these tips and tricks, such as defining your advertising goals, choosing the appropriate ad format, creating engaging content, targeting the appropriate audience, using relevant hashtags, monitoring and refining your performance, and making use of Instagram's ad features. Keep in mind that the creation of engaging content that resonates with your target audience and is in line with your advertising goals is the most important step in running a successful advertising campaign on Instagram.

Chapter 11: Creating a Content Calendar for Consistent and Engaging Posts

―――

M aking Instagram posts that are reliable and interesting requires a number of steps, one of which is developing a content calendar. You can plan and organize your content with the assistance of a content calendar, which increases the likelihood that you will post frequently and successfully on the platform. In this chapter, we will go over some helpful hints and pointers for putting together a content calendar so that your Instagram posts are consistent and interesting.

11.1. Define the Main Ideas of Your Content

The first step in developing an effective content calendar is to specify the themes that will be used for your content. Think about the different kinds of content that your audience is interested in as well as the different themes that are congruent with your brand and messaging. Define your themes by basing them on the interests of your audience as well as the principles that your brand stands for.

11.2. Determine Your Posting Schedule (Posting Schedule)

It's important to choose your posting schedule if you want to create consistent and engaging posts on Instagram, and you can do that here. Think about how frequently you want to post on the platform as well as the times of day when the majority of your audience is most active. Make use of Instagram Insights or other third-party tools to monitor the activity of your audience on the platform, and then adjust your posting schedule in accordance with this data.

11.3. Plan Your Content

It is absolutely necessary to plan out your content before attempting to create a successful content calendar. When planning out your content for the upcoming weeks or months, use your previously defined content themes in conjunction with your posting schedule. Think about using a variety of content formats, such as photos, videos, carousels, and Stories, to maintain your audience's interest in your brand and to keep them actively engaged.

11.4. Use Relevant Hashtags

It is essential to use hashtags that are relevant to your posts if you want to increase the reach of those posts on Instagram. Make use of hashtags that are pertinent to both your brand and the messages you wish to convey, as well as those that the audience you wish to reach is likely to search for on the platform. Employ a combination of widely used and more specialized hashtags to attract the attention of more people.

11.5. Include Topics That Are Currently Trending

Including topics that are currently popular in a trending topic list on your content calendar is a great way to ensure that your posts remain interesting to readers. Maintain an awareness of recent happenings and trends in your field, and look for opportunities to incorporate this information into the content you create. This can help keep your audience interested in your brand and engaged in what you have to say.

11.6 Coordinate Your Efforts with Those of Others

Collaborating with other users on Instagram is a great way to ensure that your content calendar remains interesting and up to date. Think about working together with other companies in your industry or with influential people in the field to produce content that speaks to your target demographic and promotes your company.

11.7. Keep an eye on your performance and make adjustments as necessary.

It is essential to monitor and improve your performance in order to maximize the effectiveness of your content calendar on Instagram. Track the performance of your posts by using Instagram Insights or other third-party tools to see which ones are generating the most engagement and conversions. You can improve your results on the platform by refining your content calendar using the data you collected on how well it performed.

In conclusion, developing a content calendar is an essential component of maintaining a consistent presence on Instagram through the creation of engaging posts. You can create a successful content calendar that assists you in reaching your target audience and achieving your business goals on the platform by utilizing these tips and tricks, such as defining your content themes, choosing your posting schedule, planning your content, using relevant hashtags, incorporating trending topics, collaborating with others, monitoring and refining your performance, and so on. Keep in mind that the creation of engaging and high-quality content that resonates with your target audience and is aligned with the values and messaging of your brand is the essential component of a successful content calendar.

Chapter 12: Instagram Analytics: Measuring Success and Making Improvements

———

Instagram Analytics is a powerful tool that allows you to measure the success of your marketing efforts on Instagram and make adjustments to your strategy based on those findings. You can gain valuable insights into your audience, content, and engagement on the platform by analyzing the data pertaining to your performance on the platform. In this chapter, we will go over some useful hints and suggestions for utilizing Instagram Analytics to evaluate the efficacy of your Instagram marketing strategy and identify areas for improvement.

12.1. Establish Your Objectives

The first thing you need to do before using Instagram Analytics to measure your success and make improvements is to define your goals. Think about the results you want to get from your Instagram marketing efforts, such as increasing brand awareness, driving traffic to your website, or making sales. The ability to focus your analysis and measure your progress towards achieving your business goals is facilitated by the establishment of clear goals.

12.2 Keep an Eye on Your Most Important Metrics

Tracking your performance on Instagram requires close attention to your key metrics, which you must monitor.

Tracking metrics such as engagement rate, follower growth, reach, and impressions can be done through the use of Instagram Insights or other third-party tools. Maintaining a regular monitoring schedule for your metrics will allow you to monitor your progress toward your goals and identify areas in which you can improve.

12.3. Analyze Your Audience

It is essential to conduct an audience analysis in order to gain a better understanding of who your followers are and how to more effectively target them. Tracking audience demographics such as age, gender, and location can be accomplished through the use of Instagram Insights or other third-party tools. Conduct an analysis of the data you have collected from your audience in order to discover patterns and insights that will assist you in developing content that is better targeted and more effective.

12.4. Evaluate Your Content

It is important to evaluate your content in order to gain a better understanding of the types of content that are most likely to resonate with your audience and to drive engagement. Tracking metrics such as likes, comments, and shares on your posts can be accomplished through the use of Instagram Insights or other third-party tools. Conduct an analysis of the data you have gathered about your content in order to discover patterns and trends that you can use to help you produce content that is more interesting and useful.

12.5. Keep an Eye on Your Rival Companies

It is essential to keep an eye on your rivals if you want to gain an understanding of how your brand compares to those of other companies in your sector. Tracking the activity of your rivals on Instagram can be done with the help of Instagram Insights or other third-party tools. Conduct an analysis of the data collected by your rivals in order to recognize patterns and insights that you can use to improve your own Instagram marketing strategy.

12.6 Make Adjustments to Your Strategy

It is absolutely necessary to modify your approach in light of the data provided by Instagram Analytics if you want to see improvements in your performance on the platform. Make adjustments to your content strategy, targeting, and messaging based on the performance data and audience insights you've gathered. You can continually improve your performance on the platform by putting new strategies and tactics to the test that are informed by your data.

In conclusion, integrating Instagram Analytics into your marketing strategy for Instagram is an essential step in gauging your level of success and identifying areas for improvement. You will be able to gain valuable insights into your Instagram performance and optimize your strategy to achieve your business goals on the platform if you make use of these tips and tricks, such as setting your goals, monitoring your key metrics, analyzing your audience, evaluating your content, monitoring your competitors, and refining your strategy. For example, setting your goals, monitoring your key metrics, analyzing your audience, evaluating your content, and monitoring your competitors. Keep in mind that the most important factor in determining your level of achievement on Instagram is the degree to which you consistently monitor and assess your performance data and make use of the insights gained to adjust, enhance, and perfect your strategy over time.

Chapter 13: Utilizing Instagram's Newest Features to Stay Ahead of the Game

―――

Because Instagram is always adding new features and making other changes, it is essential for businesses to keep up with the most recent industry developments and features if they want to continue to be successful on the platform and maintain user interest. In this chapter, we will go over some helpful hints and pointers for making the most of Instagram's most recent features so that you can always be one step ahead of the competition.

13.1. Instagram Reels

Users of Instagram now have the ability to create and share short-form videos on the platform thanks to a new feature called Instagram Reels. The length of a reel can be anywhere from thirty seconds to one minute, and it can contain any number of special effects and editing tools. Make use of Reels in order to generate content that is not only creatively stimulating but also meaningful to your audience and beneficial to the promotion of your brand.

13.2. Instagram Live

Instagram Now, also known as Instagram Live, is a feature that enables users to stream live video to their followers on the Instagram platform. You can connect with your audience in real time through Instagram Live and provide them with helpful insights or information regarding your brand or products when you do so. Live videos can also be saved and shared at a later time for those viewers who were unable to watch the broadcast while it was happening.

13.3. Instagram Guides

Instagram now has a feature called "Guides," which enables users to create curated collections of posts on a variety of different subjects. Create content on Instagram that is useful to your audience, full of information, that will resonate with them and provide value by using Instagram Guides. Tips, advice, or recommendations for products can all be provided in the form of guides.

13.4. Instagram Shopping

With the help of the Instagram Shopping feature, businesses are able to tag products within their posts and Stories, which in turn makes it simpler for Instagram users to make purchases directly from the app. Utilize the Instagram Shopping app to raise awareness of your wares and increase sales on the platform. This feature can be especially helpful for businesses that deal in online commerce.

13.5. Instagram Stories

Instagram Stories is a feature that enables users to share content that is either short in length or disappears after a period of 24 hours. You can promote new goods and services, share user-generated content, or show behind-the-scenes footage by using Instagram Stories. Stories can also be used in the form of polls, quizzes, or questions in order to encourage participation.

13.6. Instagram Reels Ads

Through the use of Instagram Reels Ads, companies are able to promote their goods and services through the distribution of brief video advertisements on the Instagram platform. Make use of Reels Ads to generate content that is not only engaging and creative but also resonant with your target audience and conducive to driving conversions for your company.

In conclusion, making use of the most recent features that Instagram has released is absolutely necessary if one wishes to stay ahead of the competition while also remaining relevant and engaging on the platform. You can create engaging and effective content for your audience that resonates with them and helps you achieve your business goals on Instagram by using these tips and tricks, such as using Instagram Reels, Instagram Live, Instagram Guides, Instagram Shopping, Instagram Stories, and Instagram Reels Ads. Keep in mind that the most important factor in determining whether or not you will be successful on Instagram is how well you keep up with the most recent features and trends and how well you use those features to create content that is both engaging and relevant for the audience you are trying to reach.

Chapter 14: Engaging with Your Audience on Instagram: Tips for Building Relationships

———

Building relationships with followers on Instagram and cultivating a devoted community around your brand are both important aspects of using the social media platform Instagram. You can generate a following on the platform that is more engaged and committed to your brand by replying to comments and messages, liking and sharing user-generated content, and holding giveaways or contests. In this chapter, we will go over some helpful hints and suggestions for engaging with your audience on Instagram and developing relationships with the people who follow you there.

14.1. Reply to Input, Including Messages and Comments

When it comes to engaging with your audience on Instagram, one of the most important things you can do is respond to their comments and direct messages. Be sure to respond to all of the messages and comments in a timely manner while maintaining a personal touch. This demonstrates to your followers that you appreciate the feedback they provide and that you are dedicated to developing a relationship with them.

14.2. Show your approval of user-generated content by sharing and liking it.

Engaging with your audience on Instagram can also be accomplished through the likes and shares of content that was created by other users. To make it simpler to locate user-generated content, consider implementing a branded hashtag or encouraging your followers to tag your brand in any posts they create. You can demonstrate to your followers that you value their contributions to your brand and appreciate their support by liking and sharing content that was created by other users.

14.3 Organize giveaways and competitions.

Building relationships with your audience on Instagram in a way that is both fun and engaging can be accomplished by holding giveaways or contests. Make sure that your giveaway or contest complies with Instagram's policies and guidelines by using their rules and guidelines. You can encourage participation from your followers by offering prizes or rewards that are pertinent to your brand or the message you want to convey.

14.4. Use Instagram Stories

Using Instagram Stories is a fantastic opportunity to engage with your audience in a manner that is less formal and more intimate. Make use of the Stories feature to present behind-the-scenes footage, discuss personal experiences, or advertise newly released goods or services. You can encourage engagement and feedback from your audience by providing them with interactive features, such as polls or quizzes.

14.5. Cooperate with the People Around You

Collaborating on Instagram with other brands or influencers is a fantastic way to broaden your reach and cultivate relationships with new types of users and audiences. Select partners to work with whose values and messages are congruent with those of your brand, and produce content that will resonate with the people you want to reach.

14.6 Keep an Eye on How Well You're Doing

It is essential to monitor your performance in order to gain a better understanding of how successful your engagement strategy is on Instagram. Tracking your engagement metrics on Instagram, such as likes, comments, and shares, can be done with Instagram Insights or other third-party tools. Conduct a data analysis to discover patterns and insights that can assist you in refining your engagement strategy, and then use these to inform future decisions.

In conclusion, interacting with the users who follow you on Instagram is one of the most important things you can do to cultivate a devoted following for your brand while also fostering relationships. You can create a more engaged and devoted following on the platform by utilizing these tips and tricks, such as responding to comments and messages, liking and sharing user-generated content, hosting giveaways or contests, utilizing Instagram Stories, collaborating with others, and monitoring your performance. Keep in mind that the key to achieving success on Instagram is to create genuine and personalized content that speaks to your target audience in a way that resonates with them, and that over time builds relationships with your followers.

Chapter 15: Instagram Shopping: How to Use the Platform to Sell Products

―――

With the help of the powerful Instagram Shopping feature, businesses are now able to sell their wares directly on the Instagram platform. With Instagram Shopping, companies can tag products in their posts and Stories, create a shop on their profile, and even give customers the option to purchase products directly from the application. In this chapter, we will go over some helpful hints and pointers for selling products on Instagram by utilizing the Instagram Shopping app.

15.1. Create a shopping account for yourself on Instagram.

The first thing you need to do in order to start selling products through Instagram is to create an account for Instagram Shopping. Make certain that you have a Facebook page that is connected to your Instagram account and that you have a business account on Instagram. Following the steps outlined in the Instagram app, you will be able to set up an Instagram Shopping account once you have reached this point.

15.2 Make a Storefront for Yourself on Your Profile.

When you want to sell products through Instagram Shopping, one of the most important things you need to do is set up a shop on your profile. Make it simple for customers to peruse your wares and make a purchase without leaving the app by displaying them in your profile's Shop section and making it easy to navigate. Make sure that your shop is updated on a consistent basis with new products and specials in order to maintain customer interest.

15.3 Include product tags in your social media posts and stories.

You can make use of Instagram Shopping to sell more of your products by, among other things, tagging products in your posts and Stories. Make it simple for customers to buy directly from your posts or Stories by highlighting specific products with product tags and making it easy for them to do so. When showcasing your wares, it is imperative that you make use of images of a crystal clear and high-quality product.

15.4. Use Instagram Ads

Utilizing Instagram Ads is an efficient method for marketing your products and services to a more extensive audience on the Instagram platform. Employ Instagram Ads to zero in on your ideal customer base and promote your wares with pictures and videos that grab people's attention. To increase the likelihood of people making a purchase, you should incorporate prominent calls to action and links to your online store or individual product pages.

15.5 Form Alliances with Prominent Figures

Working in conjunction with Instagram users who have a large following and a significant amount of influence is yet another productive way to use the platform to sell items. Pick influencers whose values and messages are congruent with those of your brand and who already have an engaged audience. Collaborate with people who have a large following and influence to spread the word about your products and encourage people to buy them from your online store or product pages.

15.6 Keep an Eye on Your Own Performance

It is essential to monitor your performance in order to gain an understanding of how well your Instagram Shopping strategy is functioning on the platform. Tracking your sales metrics, such as revenue and conversion rate, can be accomplished through the use of Instagram Insights or other third-party tools. Your performance data should be analyzed in order to discover patterns and insights that will assist you in improving your Instagram Shopping strategy.

In conclusion, making use of Instagram Shopping is an efficient method for selling products directly on the platform itself. You can create a successful Instagram Shopping strategy that increases sales and promotes your brand on the platform by utilizing these tips and tricks, such as setting up your Instagram Shopping account, creating a shop on your profile, tagging products in your posts and Stories, using Instagram Ads, partnering with influencers, and monitoring your performance. Keep in mind that the most important factor in determining your level of success on Instagram Shopping is the creation of high-quality and interesting content that speaks to your target demographic in a way that resonates with them and encourages them to make purchases directly from the app.

Chapter 16: Expanding Your Reach on Instagram: How to Cross-Promote on Other Platforms

P romoting your Instagram content on other platforms can be an efficient way to increase the number of people who see it and to connect with new audiences. You can drive more traffic to your Instagram profile, as well as increase the number of people following you and the amount of engagement you get on Instagram, by sharing the content you post on Instagram on other platforms, such as Facebook, Twitter, or Pinterest. In this chapter, we will go over some useful hints and suggestions for increasing your reach on Instagram as well as conducting cross-promotions on other platforms.

16.1. Publish Your Instagram Photos and Videos on Facebook.

You can easily cross-promote your content and increase your reach on both Instagram and Facebook by sharing your Instagram posts on those respective networks. Utilize the Instagram-Facebook integration so that your Facebook page will be updated with your most recent Instagram posts automatically. You are able to reach a larger audience and generate more engagement on both platforms as a result of this.

16.2. Tweet any posts you make on Instagram.

If you want to cross-promote your content and reach new audiences, one of the most effective ways to do so is to tweet your Instagram posts. You can encourage your followers to check out your Instagram profile by sharing your posts from Instagram on Twitter and linking to your profile. To ensure that your content is seen by more people, be sure to include the appropriate hashtags and mentions in your posts.

16.3 Post images from your Instagram account to Pinterest.

Pinning your Instagram photos and videos to your Pinterest boards is yet another efficient method for cross-promoting your content and reaching new audiences. Utilize Pinterest as a platform from which to showcase your Instagram posts and promote your brand. Increase the visibility of your content on Pinterest by ensuring that you use descriptive terms and keywords that are pertinent to the topic.

16.4. Use Email Marketing

Utilizing email marketing as a means of cross-promoting the content you post to Instagram and reaching new audiences is another efficient method. You can encourage your subscribers to follow your Instagram profile by using email marketing to share your Instagram posts and invite them to do so. When you send out emails, you should make sure to include links to your Instagram profile as well as clear calls to action.

16.5. Cooperate with the People Around You

Collaborating with other brands or influencers on other platforms is an efficient way to increase the number of people who see your content and to promote it in a variety of different contexts. Select partners to work with whose values and messages are congruent with those of your brand, and produce content that will resonate with the people you want to reach. You can reach new audiences, increase the number of people following you, and have more engagement if you both share each other's content on your respective platforms.

16.6. Keep an Eye on Your Own Performance.

It is essential to keep track of your performance in order to gain an understanding of how your cross-promotion strategy is performing on other platforms. Tracking your engagement metrics on other platforms, such as clicks, likes, and shares, can be accomplished with the help of analytics tools. Conduct a data analysis on your performance to search for patterns and insights that may assist you in developing and improving your cross-promotional strategy.

In conclusion, promoting your Instagram account on other platforms in order to reach new audiences and expand your reach on Instagram is an effective way to do so. You can create a successful cross-promotion strategy that drives engagement and growth on both Instagram and other platforms by utilizing these tips and tricks, such as sharing your Instagram posts on Facebook, tweeting your Instagram posts, pinning your Instagram posts on Pinterest, utilizing email marketing, collaborating with others, and monitoring your performance. Keep in mind that the most important factor in determining your level of success is the creation of content that is both engaging and relevant for your target audience. This will motivate them to follow your Instagram profile and interact with your brand over the course of time.

Chapter 17: The Dos and Don'ts of Instagram Marketing for Business

---

The use of Instagram marketing by businesses that want to build their brand, increase engagement with their customers, and boost sales can be a powerful tool. However, when approaching Instagram marketing with a clear strategy and an understanding of the platform's best practices, it is important to have both of these things in place. Dos and don'ts of marketing your business on Instagram are going to be covered in this chapter.

17.1. Make Sure to: Establish a Consistent Visual Identity for Your Brand

Developing an Instagram marketing strategy that includes the establishment of a visually identifiable brand aesthetic is essential. Create a unified look and feel for your brand on the platform by utilizing colors, fonts, and imagery that are all consistent throughout. This makes it easier for your followers to recognize your brand and boosts the overall impact of the content you produce.

17.2. Don't: Ignore Your Audience

One of the most common errors made in Instagram marketing is ignoring one's audience. Be sure to respond to people's messages and comments in a timely manner while also giving them a personal touch. This demonstrates to your followers that you appreciate the feedback they provide and that you are dedicated to developing a relationship with them.

17.3: Be Sure to Make Strategic Use of Hashtags

On Instagram, increasing the visibility of your content can be accomplished in an efficient manner by making strategic use of hashtags. Make use of hashtags that are both specific and relevant to your brand or the message you want to convey. Be sure to conduct research on the hashtags that are currently trending in your industry and incorporate them into your content in the appropriate contexts.

17.4. Don't: Overuse Hashtags

Your content on Instagram may have less of an impact if you use too many hashtags because it may appear to other users as spam. Be sure to use a combination of hashtags that are specific and relevant to your brand or the messaging you want to convey, and try to avoid using too many hashtags in a single post.

Do: Maintain a Regular Posting Schedule 17.5

When it comes to maintaining engagement and developing a dedicated following on Instagram, posting on a consistent basis is critical. Make use of a content calendar to organize and pre-schedule the posting of your content. Be sure to post on a regular basis and at times of the day when your audience is most likely to be using the platform.

17.6. Don't: Only Post Content That Is Being Promoted

If you only post promotional content to Instagram, you risk alienating your audience and seeing a decrease in engagement there. To maintain your followers' engagement and interest in your brand, you should post a combination of promotional and non-promotional content. Some examples of this type of content include behind-the-scenes footage, user-generated content, and industry news.

17.7. Make Sure to Check How Well You're Doing

It is essential to measure your performance if you want to gain an understanding of how successful your marketing strategy on Instagram is on the platform. Tracking your engagement metrics on Instagram, such as likes, comments, and shares, can be done with Instagram Insights or other third-party tools. Conduct a thorough analysis of your performance data in order to discover patterns and insights that you can use to improve your Instagram marketing strategy.

17.8. Don't Invest Money in Buying Followers or Engagement

Buying followers or engagement on Instagram is a common mistake that can be detrimental to the reputation of your brand and reduce the efficacy of your marketing efforts. Both of these problems can be avoided by avoiding these pitfalls. Concentrate on growing a real and active following on the platform by publishing content that is both of high quality and pertinent to the needs and interests of the audience you are trying to reach.

In conclusion, approaching Instagram marketing with a distinct strategy and an understanding of the platform's best practices is essential if you want to build your brand, drive engagement, and increase sales on the platform. You can create a successful Instagram marketing strategy for your business by following these dos and don'ts of using Instagram for business, such as creating a consistent brand aesthetic, using hashtags strategically, posting consistently, and measuring your performance. If you do all of these things, you will be able to create a strategy that resonates with your target audience and drives business growth.

Chapter 18: Instagram for B2B Businesses: How to Use the Platform to Reach Your Target Market

Instagram is not only for businesses that sell directly to consumers; businesses that sell to other businesses can also use the platform to connect with potential customers and reach their target market. You can use the Instagram platform to drive engagement and increase sales for your business that caters to other businesses by producing content that is relevant and engaging, focusing on your ideal audience, and making strategic use of Instagram's features. In this chapter, we will go over some helpful hints and suggestions for using Instagram for business-to-business interactions.

18.1. Define Your Target Audience

Establishing who your ideal Instagram followers are is one of the most important steps in using the platform for B2B companies. Make use of buyer personas to determine your ideal audience and gain an understanding of the challenges they face and the factors that motivate them. This makes it easier for you to create content that will resonate with your ideal audience and will drive engagement with the platform.

18.2. Use Instagram Ads

Utilizing Instagram Ads is an efficient method for reaching your ideal audience and promoting your business-to-business (B2B) goods and services on the platform. Targeting your ideal audience on Instagram can be done based on demographics, interests, or behavior if you use Instagram Ads. To increase the number of people who convert, you should ensure that your calls to action are crystal clear and that there are links leading to your website or landing pages.

18.3: Produce Content That Is Both Engaging and Relevant

The development of content that is both engaging and pertinent is an essential component of using Instagram for B2B companies. In order to showcase your products or services and provide value to your target audience, you should use messaging that is clear and visuals of a high quality. To ensure that your content is seen by as many people as possible, be sure to include captions and hashtags that are pertinent to your field and your messaging.

18.4. Use Instagram Stories

The use of Instagram Stories is an excellent method for producing content for your B2B company that is less formal and more personalized. Make use of the Stories feature to present behind-the-scenes footage, discuss personal experiences, or advertise newly released goods or services. You can encourage engagement and feedback from your audience by providing them with interactive features, such as polls or quizzes.

18.5: Distribute Content Generated by Users

Sharing user-generated content is an efficient method of showcasing your B2B products or services and building relationships with your audience on Instagram. This can be accomplished by using hashtags to search for user-generated content. You should encourage your customers to tag your company in any posts or Stories they create, and you should also share their content on your Instagram profile and Stories. This demonstrates to your audience that you are dedicated to developing a relationship with them and that you value the feedback that they provide.

18.6. Keep an Eye on Your Own Performance.

It is essential to monitor your performance in order to gain a better understanding of how well your Instagram strategy is working for your B2B company. Tracking your engagement metrics on Instagram, such as likes, comments, and shares, can be done with Instagram Insights or other third-party tools. Conduct an analysis of your performance data to discover patterns and insights that will assist you in honing your Instagram strategy and more effectively reaching the people you want to connect with.

In conclusion, utilizing Instagram for B2B businesses is a powerful tool that enables you to reach your target market and build relationships with prospective clients. You can use the platform to drive engagement and increase sales for your B2B company if you follow these tips and tricks, such as defining your target audience, using Instagram Ads, creating content that is engaging and relevant, using Instagram Stories, sharing user-generated content, and monitoring your performance.

Keep in mind that the most important factor in determining your level of success is the creation of high-quality and personalized content that connects with your intended audience and fosters long-term relationships with your followers.

Chapter 19: Building an Instagram Community: How to Foster Brand Loyalty and Repeat Business

———

Developing a sizable following on Instagram is one of the most important things you can do to expand your company's presence on the platform. You can convert your followers into loyal customers and advocates for your brand by cultivating customer loyalty to your brand and encouraging repeat business. In this chapter, we will go over some useful hints and suggestions for fostering brand loyalty and developing a community on Instagram.

19.1. Encourage Participation from Users

The development of an Instagram community relies heavily on the active participation of its users. Make use of calls-to-action in your Instagram captions and Stories to encourage your followers to interact with your content in some way, whether that be by liking, commenting, or sharing your posts. Make it a point to respond to followers' comments and direct messages in a timely and personable manner to demonstrate that you value the feedback provided by your audience.

19.2 Run competitions and give-aways on your Instagram account.

Holding Instagram contests and giving away prizes is an efficient method for fostering customer loyalty and increasing engagement with a brand. To encourage participation in your contests and giveaways from your followers, offer prizes that are both original and pertinent to your brand. To attract a larger number of participants in your giveaways and contests, you should make sure to promote them across all of your social media platforms.

19.3. Use Instagram Live

Making use of Instagram Live is a fantastic method for generating content that is both current and genuine for your Instagram community. You can use Live to host question-and-answer sessions, product demonstrations, or footage from behind the scenes of your company. You can encourage engagement and feedback from your audience by providing them with interactive features, such as polls or quizzes.

19.4: Disseminate the Content Generated by Users

Sharing user-generated content is an efficient method for showcasing your Instagram community and developing loyalists to your brand. You should encourage your followers to tag your company in any posts or Stories they create, and you should also share their content on your Instagram profile and Stories. This demonstrates to your audience that you are dedicated to developing a relationship with them and that you value the feedback that they provide.

19.5. Establish a Hashtag for Your Company

The development of a branded hashtag is an excellent method for fostering loyalty to a brand as well as encouraging user-generated content. Make use of a hashtag that is original, easy to remember, and relevant to your brand or message. You should encourage your followers to use your branded hashtag in their posts and Stories, and you should also share their content on your Instagram profile and Stories.

19.6. Give Something of Value to Your Followers

Offering incentives to people who follow your brand on social media is an efficient way to cultivate brand loyalty and encourage repeat business. Rewarding your most engaged followers can be done through the use of personalized shoutouts, early access to newly released products, or exclusive discounts. This demonstrates to your audience that you appreciate their continued support, which in turn motivates them to maintain their engagement with your brand over time.

In conclusion, cultivating an active and engaged community on Instagram is one of the most important steps in expanding your company's presence on the platform. You can cultivate brand loyalty and repeat business for your company by adhering to these tips and tricks, such as encouraging user engagement, hosting contests and giveaways on Instagram, utilizing Instagram Live, sharing user-generated content, creating a branded hashtag, and rewarding your followers. These are just some of the things you can do. Keep in mind that the most important thing you can do to achieve success on Instagram is to create content that is both personalized and engaging, so that it will resonate with your community and help you build relationships with your followers over time.

Chapter 20: Advanced Instagram Strategies: Taking Your Business to the Next Level

When you have a firm grasp on the fundamentals of marketing your business on Instagram, it is time to take your strategy to the next level by incorporating more advanced strategies and methods. In this chapter, we will talk about advanced strategies for Instagram that can help you grow your business, increase engagement, and differentiate yourself from the other businesses in your industry.

20.1. Engage in Marketing Based on Influence

Increase both your reach and the number of people engaging with your content on Instagram by making use of influencer marketing. Work together with influential people in your field to spread the word about your company's goods and services among their respective audiences. If you want your influencer marketing campaign to have the greatest possible impact, you should select influencers who have a following that is both active and genuine.

20.2. Create Instagram Guides

Providing your audience with content that is helpful and educational can now be accomplished in an innovative and efficient way thanks to the creation of Instagram Guides. You can share advice about your industry, tutorials about your products, or user-generated content by using Instagram Guides. To reach a greater number of people, you should make sure to promote your Instagram Guides across all of your other social media platforms.

20.3. Use Instagram Reels

Making use of Instagram Reels is an excellent method for generating short-form content that is engaging for your audience. You can use Reels to showcase your products or services, provide advice or trends for the industry, or showcase footage from behind the scenes. Make your reels stand out from the rest of the pack by utilizing music and effects that are creative and easy to remember.

20.4. Spend Money on Photographers Who Are Professionals

Making an investment in professional photography is a great way to improve the overall quality of your Instagram content and to increase its impact. You can increase engagement on the platform by showcasing your products or services with images of high quality and visual appeal by using those images. Be sure to use the same branding and messaging throughout all of your photographs to ensure that your company's products and services have a unified and easily recognizable appearance.

20.5. Use Instagram Shopping

Utilizing Instagram Shopping is a powerful tool that can be utilized for the purpose of driving sales and conversions on the platform. Make the process of shopping easier for your audience by using Instagram Shopping to tag your products in your posts or Stories and providing a streamlined shopping experience. Make sure that your product descriptions and images are optimized so that you can see an increase in the number of conversions.

20.6. Host Instagram Takeovers

Instagram Takeovers are an excellent way to generate new and interesting content for your audience, and hosting one is simple to do. Make use of guest hosts who are interesting and relevant to your audience to take over your Instagram account for a predetermined amount of time. If you want to reach more people with your Instagram Takeovers, be sure to promote them on all of your other social media platforms as well.

In conclusion, putting advanced Instagram strategies to work for your business is a potent way to take it to the next level on the platform. You can increase your reach and engagement on Instagram and stand out from the competition if you follow these tips and tricks, such as using influencer marketing, creating Instagram Guides, utilizing Instagram Reels, investing in professional photography, utilizing Instagram Shopping, and hosting Instagram Takeovers. Always keep in mind that the most important factor in determining your level of success is the ability to produce unique and interesting content that strikes a chord with your intended readers and fosters long-term relationships with those readers.

Also by B. Vincent

Affiliate Marketing
Affiliate Marketing
Affiliate Marketing

Standalone
Business Employee Discipline
Affiliate Recruiting
Business Layoffs & Firings
Business and Entrepreneur Guide
Business Remote Workforce
Career Transition
Project Management
Precision Targeting
Professional Development
Strategic Planning
Content Marketing
Imminent List Building
Getting Past GateKeepers
Banner Ads

Bookkeeping
Bridge Pages
Business Acquisition
Business Bogging
Business Communication Course
Marketing Automation
Better Meetings
Business Conflict Resolution
Business Culture Course
Conversion Optimization
Creative Solutions
Employee Recruitment
Startup Capital
Employee Incentives
Employee Mentoring
Followership
Servant Leadership
Human Resources
Team Building
Freelancing
Funnel Building
Geo Targeting
Goal Setting
Immanent List Building
Lead Generation
Leadership Course
Leadership Transition
Leadership vs Management
LinkedIn Ads
LinkedIn Marketing
Messenger Marketing

New Management
Newsfeed Ads
Search Ads
Online Learning
Sales Webinars
Side Hustles
Split Testing
Twitter Timeline Advertising
Earning Additional Income Through Side Hustles: Begin
Earning Money Immediately
Making a Living Through Blogging: Earn Money Working
From Home
Create Bonuses for Affiliate Marketing: Your Success Is
Encompassed by Your Bonuses
Internet Marketing Success: The Most Effective
Traffic-Driving Strategies
JV Recruiting: Joint Ventures Partnerships and Affiliates
Secrets to List Building
Step-by-Step Facebook Marketing: Discover How To Create
A Strategy That Will Help You Grow Your Business
Banner Advertising: Traffic Can Be Boosted by Banner Ads
Affiliate Marketing
Improve Your Marketing Strategy with Internet Marketing
Outsourcing Helps You Save Time and Money
Choosing the Right Content and Marketing for Social Media
Make Products That Will Sell
Launching a Product for Affiliate Marketing
Pinterest as a Marketing Tool
Banner Blitz: Mastering the Art of Advertising with
Eye-Catching Banners

Beyond Commissions: Maximizing Affiliate Profits with Creative Bonus Strategies

Retargeting Mastery: Winning Sales with Online Strategies

Power Partnerships: Mastering the Art of Business Growth Through Partnership Recruiting

The List Advantage: Unlocking the Power of List Building for Marketing Success

Capital Catalyst: The Essential Guide to Raising Funds for Your Business

Mobile Mastery: The Ultimate Guide to Successful Mobile Marketing Campaigns

Crowdfunding Secrets: A Comprehensive Guide to Successfully Funding Your Next Project

Insta-Brand: The Ultimate Guide to Growing Your Business on Instagram

About the Publisher

Accepting manuscripts in the most categories. We love to help people get their words available to the world.

Revival Waves of Glory focus is to provide more options to be published. We do traditional paperbacks, hardcovers, audio books and ebooks all over the world. A traditional royalty-based publisher that offers self-publishing options, Revival Waves provides a very author friendly and transparent publishing process, with President Bill Vincent involved in the full process of your book. Send us your manuscript and we will contact you as soon as possible.

Contact: Bill Vincent at rwgpublishing@yahoo.com

Printed by BoD˝in Norderstedt, Germany